Wild West Scroll Saw Portraits

By Gary Browning

Fox Chapel Publishing Co. Inc.

1970 Broad Street • East Petersburg, PA 17520 • www.foxchapelpublishing.com

Dedication
To my friend and brother Harry and to Gordon who will be missed
but will always be looking down on us.

Publisher: Alan Giagnocavo
Project Editor: Ayleen Stellhorn
Layout and Design: Alan Davis
Cover Design: Keren Holl
Interior Photography: Tim Mize

ISBN # 1–56523–186–4
Library of Congress Preassigned Card Number: 2002102660

To order your copy of this book,
please send check or money order
for the cover price plus $3.50 shipping to:
Fox Books
1970 Broad Street
East Petersburg, PA 17520

Or visit us on the web at
www.foxchapelpublishing.com

Printed in China

10   9   8   7   6   5   4   3   2

Because scrolling wood and other materials inherently includes the risk of injury and damage, this book cannot guarantee that creating the projects in this book is safe for everyone. For this reason, this book is sold without warranties or guarantees of any kind, express or implied, and the publisher and author disclaim any liability for any injuries, losses or damages caused in any way by the content of this book or the reader's use of the tools needed to complete the projects presented here. The publisher and the author urge all scrollers to thoroughly review each project and to understand the use of all tools involved before beginning any project.

Table of Contents

*I*ntroduction

I started portrait scrolling in 1995. I had been scrolling off and on for a couple of years before that, but my "awakening" happened in 1995. I say awakening because when I first started I scrolled only now and then and I did not really have a lot of interest in seeing what the common tool could actually be used for. I bought the scroll saw on a whim because it looked like a simple tool that could be handy for many things. The scroll saw proved to be a great asset. It also pulled some hidden talents that I did not know I had to the surface.

When I first started to manipulate photographs of family members it was trying. It took a long time to figure out how to make the patterns look natural and how to use my computer program to better aid my efforts. I took a picture with my 35-millimeter camera, made a pattern, and cut it out on my scroll saw— it looked good to me. I showed family members and they could not believe what I had done. Their praise and support have caused me to dig deeper into working on patterns and to develop an easier way of making a portrait that others could use and learn from.

I feel that the actual cutting of the portrait is the fun part. Getting the pattern to the point of being ready to use as a template for the wood is the part that is magic and will make the portrait a masterpiece or a great piece of art. It's one thing to use a pre-made pattern and follow the lines with your scroll saw, but it is truly rewarding to be a part of the making of a pattern from start to finish. When the piece is cut out and you stand back and look at it, you feel a sense of accomplishment that you are proud to share and show off. I knew that any scroller who took the time to work with it could adapt this portrait method.

Like many scroll saw enthusiasts, I find scrolling very relaxing and good therapy for the soul. It takes you away from the real world and puts you in a state of anticipation, and it drives you to complete the project so you can call it your own. Scroll sawing will always be around. Like a passionate hobby, scroll sawing will continue to give people the tool to ease their troubles and escape the daily grind. I try to tell everyone I meet how scroll sawing interests me, and I show them my work and tell them how great and rewarding it is. It is a good thing to have something in your life that will continue to give you positive results for your hard efforts.

The scroll saw communities out there are some of the best in the world. Never have I met a kinder body of people who are willing to help one another with their struggles and curiosity in their use of the scroll saw. For the most part they are good and honest people who want to share knowledge and techniques. I am honored that scrollers appreciate my work and I hope to hold their interest in future works.

-Gary Browning

Basic Cutting Instructions

Scrolled portraits are a fascinating way to capture images of people in wood. My technique, and the technique I will describe here, is to scroll the silhouetted image of a person, animal or object in light-colored wood. The actual image is removed and the remaining piece of wood is mounted on a black background. The subject's silhouette then shows in black and is very distinct against the light-colored wood. The technique also works well in reverse, where the wood around the silhouette is removed, leaving the light-colored figure silhouetted against the dark background.

At first glance, some of the patterns may seem very complex. Any pattern can be made easier by lessening the number of cutouts or by making the cutouts larger. Be sure to test any pattern alterations with a pencil and paper to ensure that your final design will cut correctly on the scroll saw.

Wood Selection

I prefer $1/8$-inch or $1/4$-inch birch or oak plywood. This type of plywood is readily available at your local home improvement store or lumber yard. This thin wood scrolls easily and is strong enough to hold the thin and sometimes fragile cuts involved in portrait scrolling.

Well-treated wood will not require any stain or paint, though you may choose to lightly sand the finished piece to remove burs and stray pattern lines. The thin plywood fits very nicely into a standard glass-covered picture frame—an ideal way to display the final piece. Its light color is also ideal against a dark felt background.

Try cutting two or three pieces of plywood at the same time to yield multiple copies of the same pattern. Stack the wood evenly and secure them with small brads or staples placed in the corners of the stack.

Blade Selection

I use a spiral blade on all my portrait work. I find this type of blade allows me to move the wood smoothly along the sometimes intricate lines of a portrait pattern. It also moves extremely fast, cutting down on the amount of time needed to scroll a piece.

If you are not familiar with using a spiral blade, be sure to practice first on a piece of scrap wood. Its operation is quite different than a traditional blade, and you may need some practice time before you become comfortable using it. Try moving the wood backward, forward, left and right while cutting. Try not to rotate the wood clockwise or counter-clockwise. Practice this exercise until you are comfortable with the feel of the blade.

Pattern Transfer

If you are using a computer to scan and copy a pattern from this book, simply print the image to standard white copy paper. More advanced computer users may want to try printing patterns on iron-on transfer paper, acetate sheets or heavy-weight paper. Traditional artists will want to use tracing paper or a photocopier to copy the patterns in this book.

I have found through experience that tracing the final pattern to the wood using carbon paper is most efficient for both computer-generated and traditionally copied patterns. Gluing the pattern to the wood works well for simple patterns; however, the spiral blade has a tendency to pick up the paper on tight turns, often tearing the paper and making the pattern useless. If you do choose to glue the pattern to the wood, be sure to spray the paper and not the wood. This will make the pattern easier to remove.

Display

I always use black felt for the background of my scroll-sawed portraits. You may also want to try using a piece of wood. Different types of material will give your finished portrait a different look. You may also want to experiment with colors other than black

I frame my finished pieces to give them the appearance of beautifully painted silhouettes. The glass also helps to protect the finished portrait from dust and fingerprints of over-anxious viewers. I buy my frames at a local discount store. A 10 x 13 frame can be purchased complete with glass, matting and backing material for much less than I could assemble one myself.

©Gary Browning

Soaring Eagle

© Gary Browning

Bald Eagle Portrait

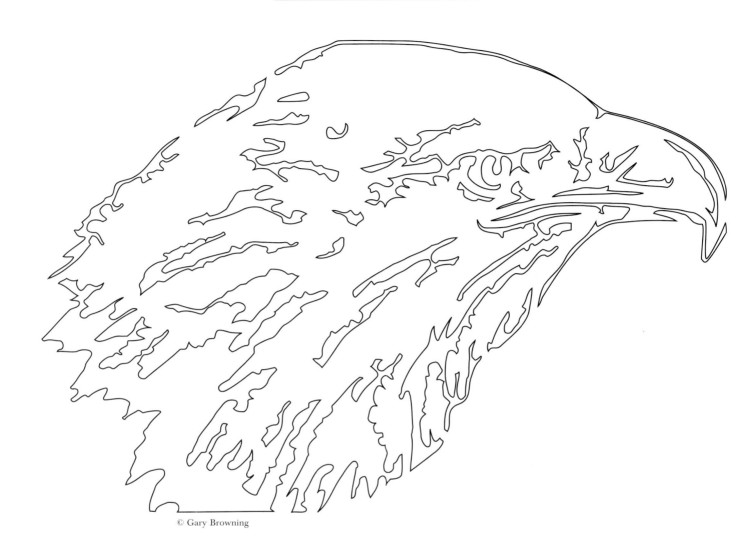

© Gary Browning

© Gary Browning

© Gary Browning

Buck Portrait

© Gary Browning

Woodland Clash

© Gary Browning

Moose Portrait

© Gary Browning

Long Horn Steer

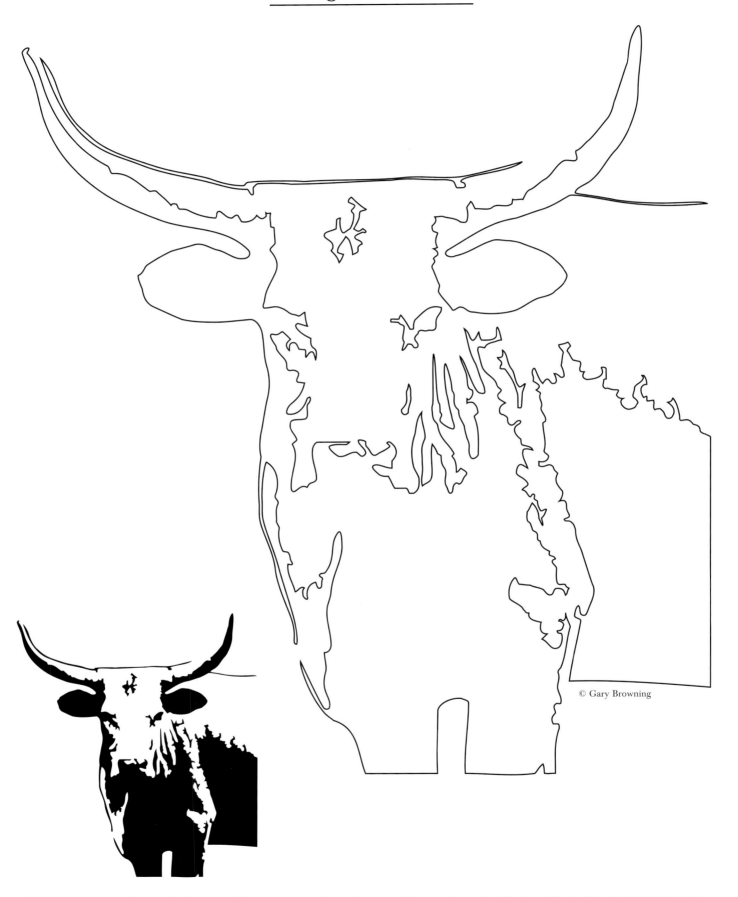

© Gary Browning

© Gary Browning

Wild Mustang

© Gary Browning

Jack Rabbit

© Gary Browning

Prairie Dog

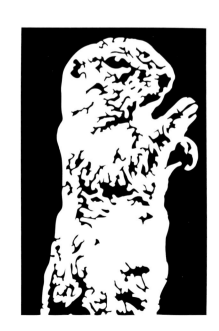

Howling Coyote

© Gary Browning

Coyote Portrait

© Gary Browning

Wolf on the Run

© Gary Browning

Fighting Bear

© Gary Browning

In the Saddle

© Gary Browning

Bronc Buster

© Gary Browning

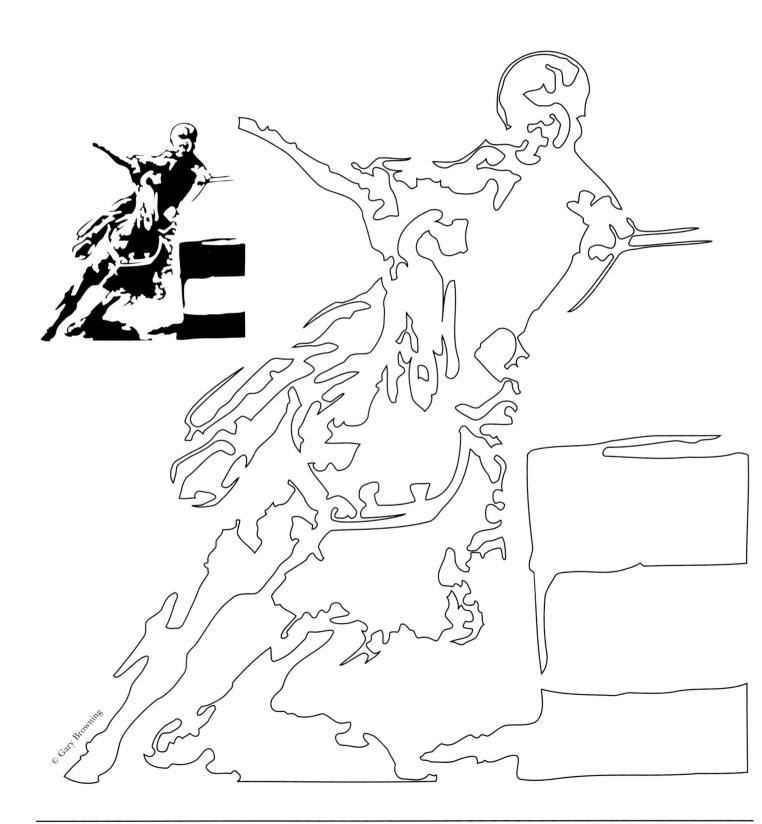

© Gary Browning

Bull Rider

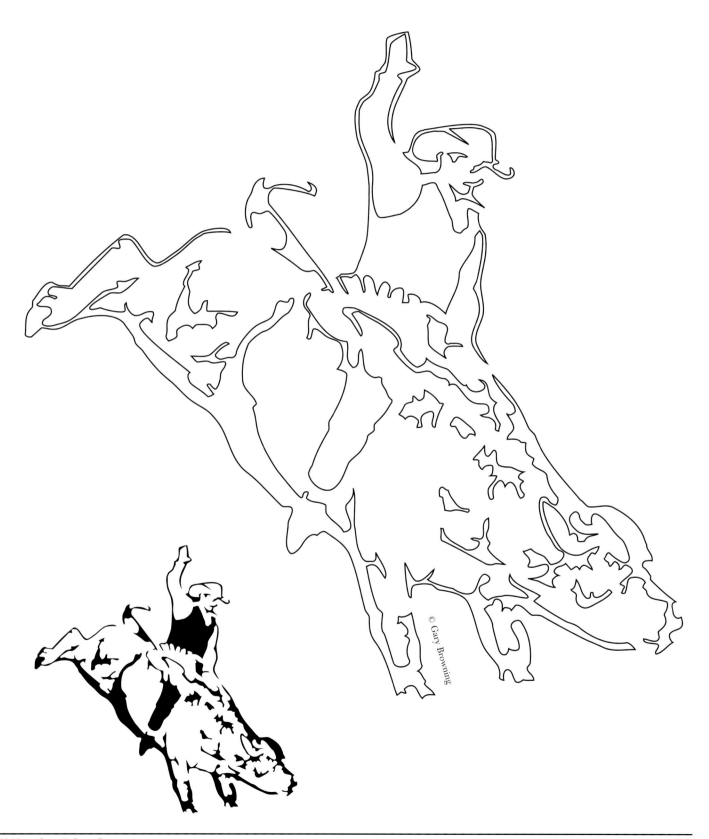

© Gary Browning

Steer Roper

© Gary Browning

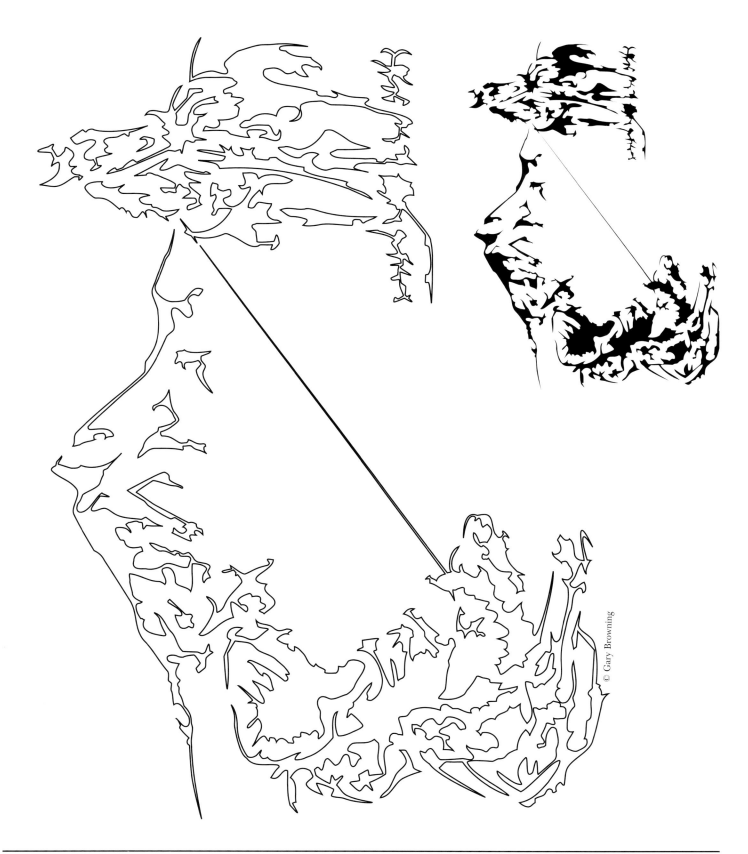

© Gary Browning

Quanah Parker

© Gary Browning

Chief Crazy Horse

Chief Little Crow

© Gary Browning

Ode to the Buffalo

by Gary Browning

Pattern on page 57

Wild Mustang
by Gary Browning

Pattern on page 13

"Poker Alice"
by Gary Browning

Pattern on page 48

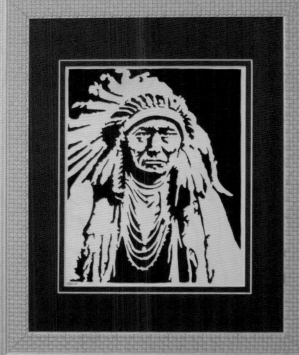

Chief Joseph
by Gary Browning

Pattern on page 37

Quanah Parker
by Gary Browning

Pattern on page 26

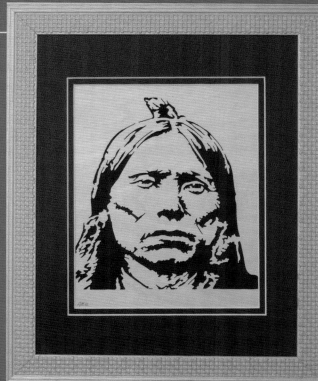

Howling Coyote
by Gary Browning

Pattern on page 16

Steer Roper
by Gary Browning

Pattern on page 24

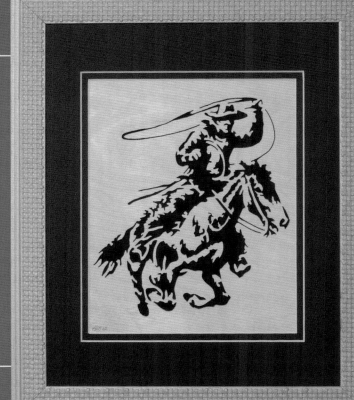

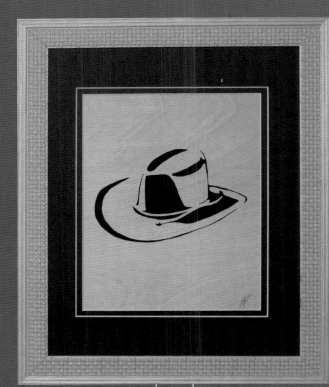

Cowboy Hat
by Gary Browning

Pattern on page 54

Heck Thomas
by Gary Browning

Pattern on page 50

Wolf on the Run
by Gary Browning

Pattern on page 18

In the Saddle
by Gary Browning

Pattern on page 20

Cowboy Boot
by Gary Browning

Pattern on page 53

Buffalo Bill
by Gary Browning

Pattern on page 43

Saddle
by Gary Browning

Pattern on page 56

American Bison Portrait
by Gary Browning

Pattern on page 5

Bald Eagle Portrait
by Gary Browning

Pattern on page 4

Butch Cassidy
by Gary Browning

Pattern on page 42

Bull Rider
by Gary Browning

Pattern on page 23

Soaring Eagle
by Gary Browning

Pattern on page 3

Mare and Foal
by Gary Browning

Pattern on page 12

Chief Joseph

© Gary Browning

Geronimo with Rifle

© Gary Browning

Geronimo

© Gary Browning

Red Cloud

© Gary Browning

Sitting Bull

© Gary Browning

Butch Cassidy

© Gary Browning

Buffalo Bill

© Gary Browning

Billy the Kid

© Gary Browning

Jesse James

© Gary Browning

Tom Smith

© Gary Browning

Wild Bill Hickock

© Gary Browning

"Poker Alice" Ivers

© Gary Browning

Doc Holiday

© Gary Browning

Heck Thomas

© Gary Browning

Jim Bridger

© Gary Browning

Poncho Villa

© Gary Browning

Cowboy Boot

© Gary Browning

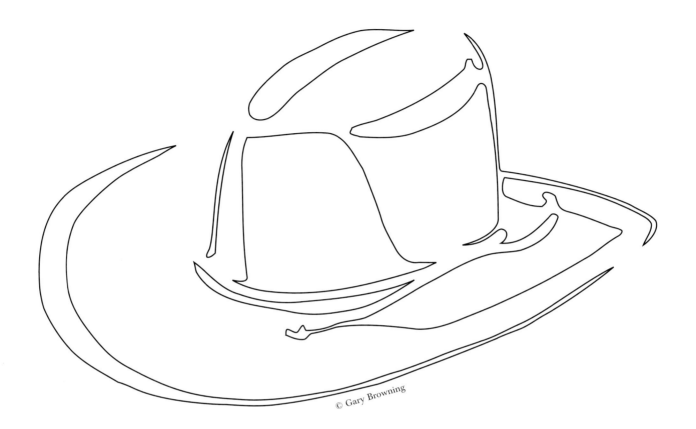

© Gary Browning

Pistol

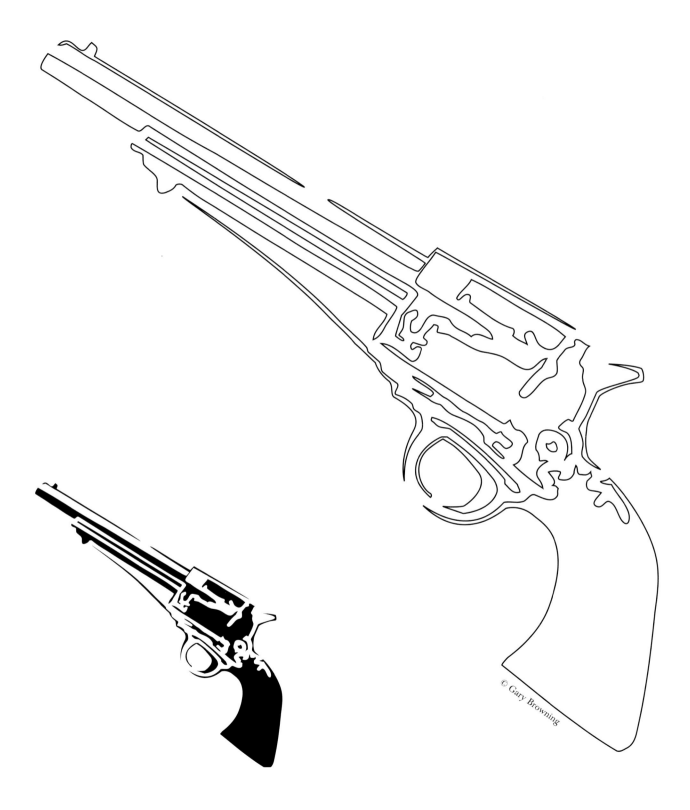

© Gary Browning

Saddle

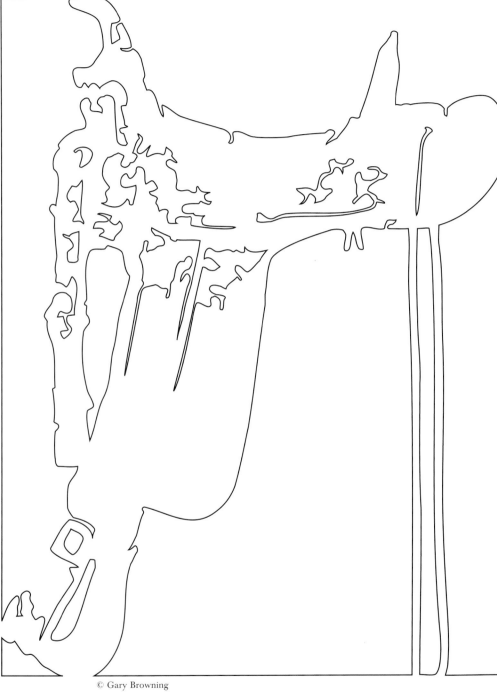

© Gary Browning

Buffalo Skull

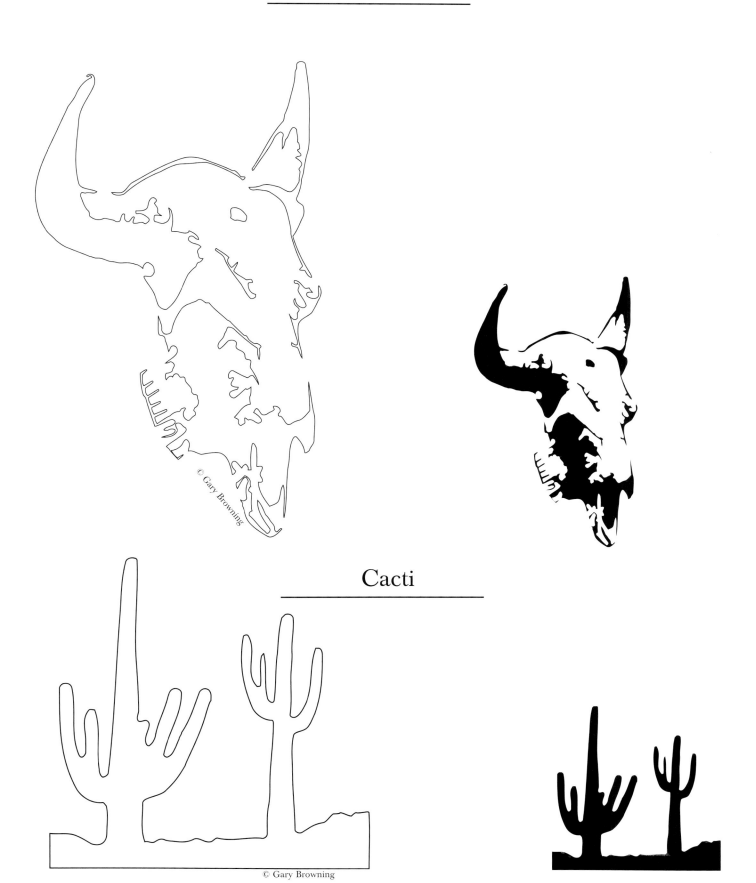

Cacti

© Gary Browning

Teepee

© Gary Browning

Tomahawks

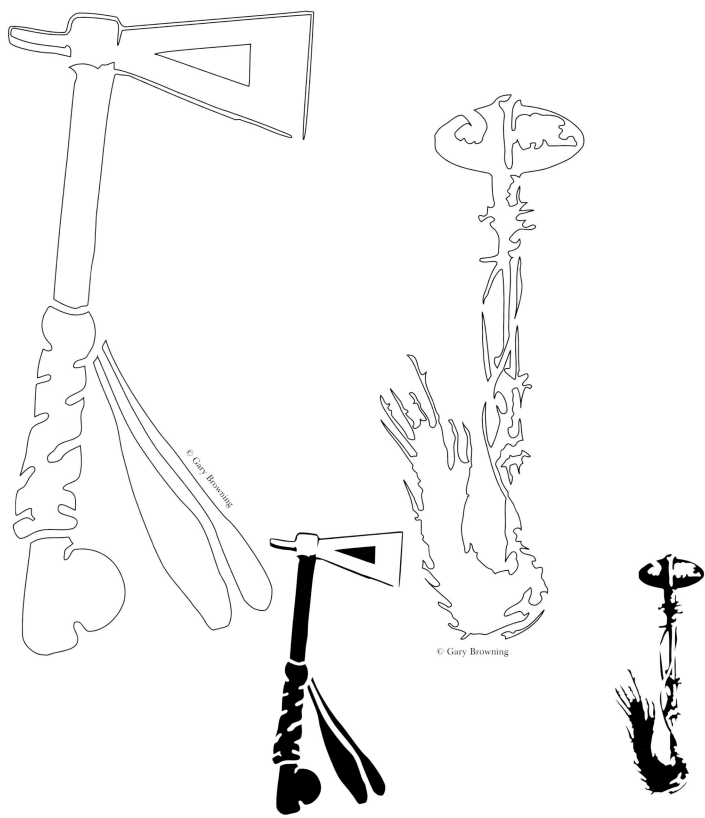

© Gary Browning

© Gary Browning

© Gary Browning

Landscapes

© Gary Browning

© Gary Browning

Buffalo Silhouette

Feather Headdress

© Gary Browning

© Gary Browning

Stylized Eagle Border

© Gary Browning

Spear Border

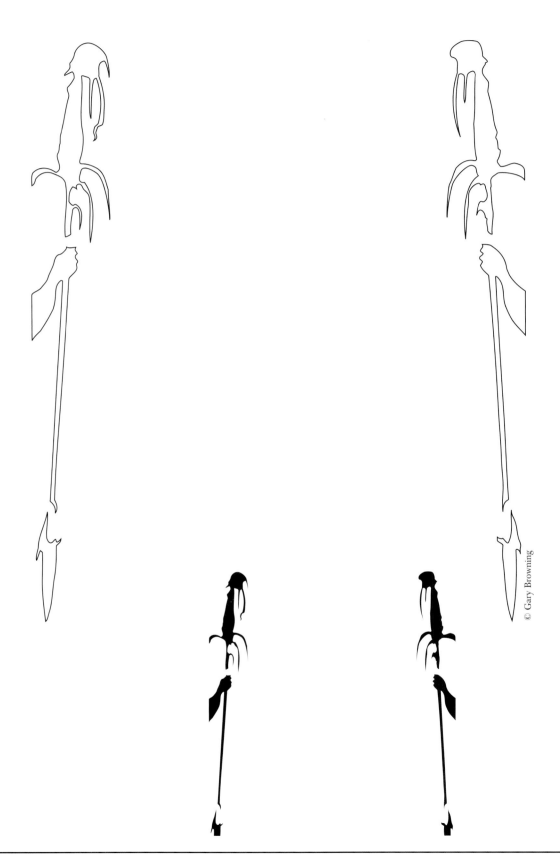

Gold Digger Border

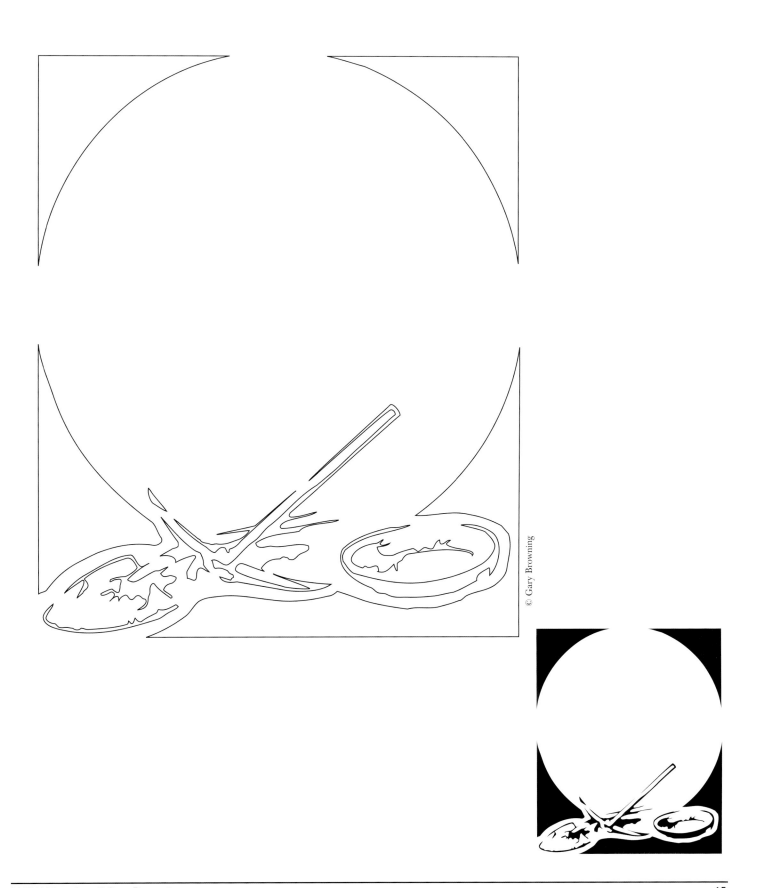

© Gary Browning

Western-Style Border

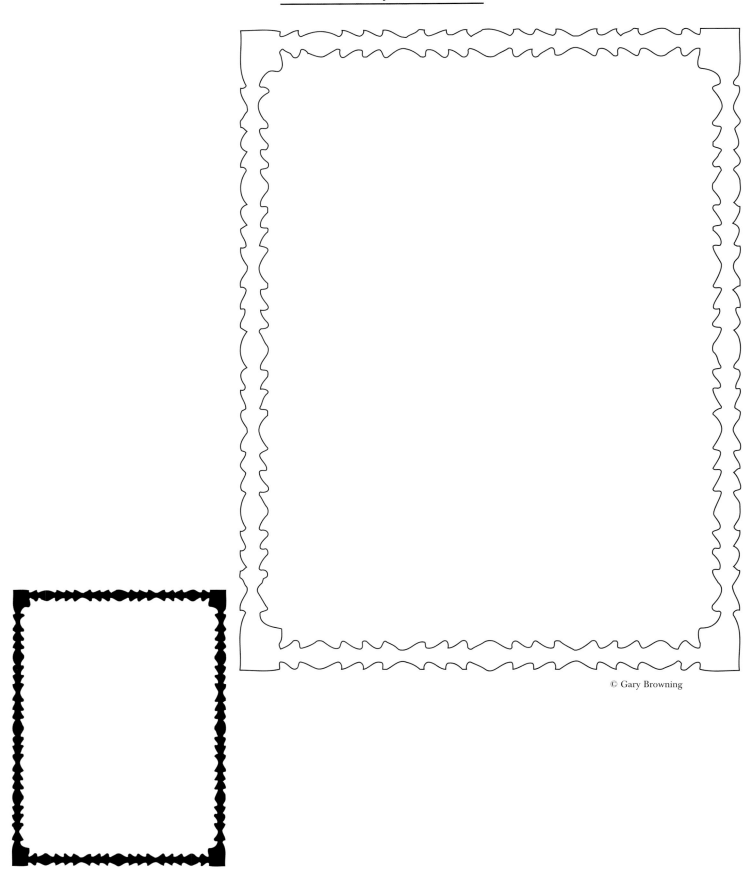

© Gary Browning

Barbed Wire Border

© Gary Browning

More Great Project Books from Fox Chapel Publishing

- **Scroll Saw Portraits by Gary Browning:** Learn how to use a computer or photocopier to change any photograph into a pattern for your scroll saw. Includes pattern-making techniques, tips on which photos make good patterns, and 55 portrait patterns.
ISBN: 1-56523-147-3, 96 pages, soft cover, $14.95

- **North American Wildlife Patterns for the Scroll Saw by Lora S. Irish:** Bring North American animals to life with the exciting scroll saw patterns found in this book. Choose from more than 50 ready-to-cut patterns that include everything from squirrels, raccoons and rabbits to moose, cougars and rams. Each pattern is drawn with crisp, easy-to-follow lines.
ISBN: 1-56523-165-1, 72 pages, soft cover, $12.95.

- **Scroll Saw Farm Puzzles by Tony and June Burns:** You'll be scrolling delightful, colorful, wooden puzzles honoring America's heartland and farm animals in no time with the ready-to-use patterns and instruction in this book! When cut, the puzzles can stand on their own, or together—creating a 30-piece barnyard scene!
ISBN: 1-56523-138-4, 72 pages, soft cover, $14.95.

- **Scroll Saw Holiday Puzzles by Tony and June Burns:** You'll be scrolling throughout the year with this festive collection of scroll saw puzzles for the holidays! From New Year's Eve and Christmas to Valentine's Day, Easter, and Halloween, you'll find over 25 delightful puzzle patterns for over 15 holidays and seasons. Basic scrolling information such as choosing a blade, safety and tips also included!
ISBN: 1-56523-204-6, 72 pages, soft cover, $14.95.

- **Dinosaur Puzzles for the Scroll Saw by Judy and Dave Peterson:** Make 30 spectacular dinosaur puzzles–from the terrifying T-Rex to the wading Brontosaurus. Features 30 puzzles and how-to instructions. Puzzles can be made with many pieces for adults or fewer pieces for children.
ISBN: 1-56523-184-8, 72 pages, soft cover, $14.95.

- **Scroll Saw Workbook 2nd Edition by John A. Nelson:** The ultimate beginner's scrolling guide! Hone your scroll saw skills to perfection with the 25 skill-building chapters and projects included in this book. Techniques and patterns for wood and non-wood projects!
ISBN: 1-56523-207-0, 88 pages, soft cover, $14.95.

- **Intarsia Workbook by Judy Gale Roberts:** Learn the art of intarsia from the #1 expert, Judy Gale Roberts! You'll be amazed at the beautiful pictures you can create when you learn to combine different colors and textures of wood to make raised 3-D images. Features 7 projects and expert instruction. Great for beginners!
ISBN: 1-56523-226-7, 72 pages, soft cover, $14.95.

- **The Complete Guide to Making Wooden Clocks 2nd Edition by John A. Nelson:** This classic book includes all you need to know to make beautiful wooden clocks in your own workshop–and now this second edition has a lower cover price. Inside, find a history of clocks in America, plans and instructions for 37 projects, and a special step-by-step project to get you started. Features plans for beginners and advanced woodworkers.
ISBN: 1-56523-208-9, 184 pages, soft cover, $19.95.

- **Woodworker's Guide to Making Traditional Mirrors and Picture Frames by John A. Nelson:** A sourcebook of patterns for woodworkers that features plans for mirrors and frames. Learn the basics behind cutting wood for mirrors and frames, and then use the included measured drawings to create your own.
ISBN: 1-56523-223-2, 112 pages, soft cover, $17.95.

- **Words of Faith in Wood by Jeff Paxton:** Learn to express your faith in wood with the 76 inspirational scroll saw patterns included in this book! This book focuses on combining actual Scripture verses with artistic imagery. The result is a lasting piece of artwork that makes a meaningful decoration for your own home, or someone else's.
ISBN 1-56523-228-3, 72 Pages, soft cover, $14.95.

CHECK WITH YOUR LOCAL WOODWORKING STORE OR BOOK RETAILER
Or call 800-457-9112 • Visit www.foxchapelpublishing.com